ORIENTAL IRON-ON TRANSFER PATTERNS

24 Authentic Embroidery Motifs from The Textile Museum

LILO MARKRICH

Drawings by Louise Craven

Dover Publications, Inc.
New York

Published in Canada by General Publishing Company, Ltd., 30
Lesmill Road, Don Mills, Toronto, Ontario.

*Oriental Iron-on Transfer Patterns. 24 Authentic Embroidery
Motifs from The Textile Museum* is a new work, first published by
Dover Publications Inc., in 1980.

International Standard Book Number: 0-486-23886-5
Library of Congress Catalog Card Number: 79-53931

Manufactured in the United States of America
Dover Publications, Inc.
31 East 2nd Street
Mineola, N.Y. 11501

Introduction

The transfer designs in this book are all adapted from actual Chinese and Japanese woven or embroidered fabrics mainly in the collection of The Textile Museum in Washington D. C.

Until the 6th century A.D., the production of silk was China's secret. Along ancient overland trails, traders brought textiles more precious than gold from the Far East to the West. The colors of these woven and embroidered silks shimmered. They felt soft to the touch, and their threads were as fine as spider webs. Their patterns were graceful, flowing and of exotic design. It is said that the Roman society's eagerness to own such costly textiles contributed to the financial decline and ultimate collapse of the empire.

In the 17th century, Europe began regular trade with the Orient. Chinese brocades, damask, and tapestry-woven (k'o-ssu) and embroidered textiles were shipped by Dutch, English and Portuguese companies from their Far Eastern trading stations to their home ports. As shipping increased, larger boats were commissioned, traveling time was cut, cargo holds were enlarged and transportation costs declined. Within a century, all of Europe was fascinated by Chinoiserie. Translucent porcelain (china), furnishings, plants, extraordinary ornaments and a never-ending flow of textiles especially designed for export became familiar throughout large areas of the West.

In China, the traditional use of silk prevailed. The ownership of fine textiles continued to indicate social rank and to mark a family's secular and religious occasions. In palaces, temples and prosperous households quality textiles were as highly valued as fine jewels. Each piece had a function and its design conformed to symbolic rules. To the artist/designer of a special embroidered textile, ancestral traditions were not restrictive but presented a creative challenge. The fruits and flowers, animals, crashing waves and jagged rocks so fascinating to the Western eye were the visual alphabet of a symbolic language he knew well. When he combined his inner vision with his fine draftsmanship, he provided an unparalleled guideline for the sophisticated and intensively trained embroiderer.

The professional embroiderer's understanding of silk as a background material and embroidery thread was based on the experience of generations. He and his work force recognized its strength, compensated for its weaknesses and understood precisely how each stitch should be adjusted to its light-reflecting properties. Without the embroiderer's craftsmanship, the artist's vision could not become reality. Some embroiderers were also designers; others used cut rice paper patterns.

Few stitches were used, and all can be found in ancient ethnographic textiles. They never overwhelm the design but instead reinforce it. In China, the dominant stitch used is known today as the satin stitch. The stitch is straight and flat. By changing its direction, the embroiderer varied the light reflection of the silks and thereby extended the shading range of a color. This needlework technique was particularly suited for the smooth spun-silk floss which was the standard needlework thread used. Satin stitch application varied.

Grouped Satin Stitch. Stitch slant was either vertical, horizontal or diagonal, and the slant depended upon whether the embroiderer wanted to broaden or elongate a shape.

"Encroached" Satin Stitch. After the first row of correctly slanted stitches had been worked, the second and all subsequent rows were started just below the finish of the previous line of stitching with the needle surfacing between two already worked stitches. The embroiderer was aware that the beginning of each new stitch would eventually be obscured by the floss spread of the two worked adjoining stitches. This method assured uninterrupted color flow but the effect was stylized.

"Long and Short" Stitch. This subtle and elegant technique (also known as needlepainting embroidery) is perhaps China's greatest contribution to needlework as an art form. Again the embroiderer had to judge the most appropriate direction of stitch flow for each segment of a motif, and this was then filled with closely worked satin stitches of varying lengths. No two contiguous stitches were of identical size. Each was either shorter or longer than its predecessor. Each stitch glided forward, away from the embroiderer. By changing color with the help of overlapped and encroaching stitches, the embroiderer used the silk floss in the same way an artist uses watercolors.

For needlepoint enthusiasts, Chinese gauze embroidery is of special interest. Vertical and horizontal satin stitches were moved in and out of the clearly visible holes. The straight flat stitches filled the shapes in a geometric manner and stitch length was adjusted as needed. Larger areas were often filled with alternating, even-sized stitches (brick stitch), with individual stitches often no longer than one-eighth of an inch.

Five other stitches are to be found in Chinese textiles worked before the first quarter of the 19th century. These are stem, split, chain, gilt thread couching and a knotted stitch known as the Pekinese or forbidden stitch. The first three were all used in an identical manner. They are linear stitches and move forward rather than sideways as in the manner of a satin stitch. Their effect is a continuous line of color. The Chinese used these stitches in two different ways.

In the first method, the stitching began at the base of a motif and this was then outlined. After the first row had been completed, instead of discontinuing the line, the needleworker continued working a spaced parallel line inside the first line. The stitch line was complete when the center had been reached. With this method a shape was defined and stylized and the visible background color was made more obvious by the lines of silk floss stitching.

The second method filled shapes with color. The stitch lines were again parallel to one another but close together and covered the background material. The use of color varied. For such motifs as waves, each line of color used was carefully evaluated to heighten the effect of movement. For flat, stylized interpretation, the lines were also worked close together, but the coloring graduated from dark to light or from light to dark.

Gilt thread couching was used in the same manner as the three linear stitches. It also had an additional use. Couched metal or gilded rice paper, spiraled around a core of silk thread, was used to outline previously silk-worked areas, providing additional richness to the work. Other silk couching had a different application. Faces, hands or large areas were filled with long stitches of a heavier than usual floss. Facial details were then stitched into the first layer of floss with finer silk thread, using tighter tension. Brows and cheeks would then appear slightly puffed. Using the same system and satin stitches, large areas were covered with geometric repeat patterns in contrasting silks. Variations are unlimited, color combinations sophisticated, and the process must have been a fascinating challenge to the worker.

The forbidden stitch or Peking knot was concave and light-reflecting. Minute in size, it eventually caused a worker's blindness. Lines of knots were worked in the manner of the linear stitches and color use was equally systematic. The first row was darker or lighter, the inner area the opposite. Gilded couched outlines always framed designs worked in this manner.

The following suggestions should be considered before the designs are interpreted by the modern needleworker.

Only the finest of materials were used in these fabrics; one must choose contemporary embroidery materials with great care. A synthetic fabric with a silk finish or a cotton satin as background material for free-form embroidery will handle more easily than an expensive lightweight pure silk. When stranded cottons or silks are used as silk floss substitutes, it is important to remember that a previously worked stitch will appear unevenly split if a needle is haphazardly brought up from the back to the front. Obvious splits will detract from the overall smoothness of encroaching satin or long and short stitching. The use of fine English crewel embroidery wool as a substitute for silk floss is not inappropriate. Seventeenth- and eighteenth-century women unable to afford silk worked many Far Eastern designs with wool on linen. Wool stitches "spread" in the same manner as silk floss worked stitches. The additional use of textured stitches not commonly found in Chinese work will detract from the elegant simplicity of the motifs.

Transferring the designs to your fabric is a fairly simple procedure. Here are directions for using these transfer patterns.

Prepare the Fabric. If the fabric is washable, preshrink and remove the sizing by laundering first. Iron carefully to remove all wrinkles. If the fabric ravels badly, it is a good idea to whip the edges by hand with an overcast stitch or to run a large zigzag machine stitch along the edges. Since transfers are made with very high temperatures which might melt synthetic fabrics, use a natural fabric such as cotton or linen. If you are unsure of the fibers in your fabric, test the ironability of the fabric first.

Prepare the Ironing Board. To prevent the motif from transferring to your ironing board, place an old sheet or other smooth fabric over the ironing board cover. To obtain a stronger impression of the pattern—especially after the transfer has been used, or on darker fabrics—place a piece of aluminum foil on your board before pressing.

Make a Test Transfer. Before beginning any project, it is a good idea to test your iron, the fabric and the evenness of your hand pressure. Cut out one of the motifs marked "Test Pattern" and follow the directions below for making a transfer. If the ink transferred well, you can proceed; if not, adjust either the heat or the length of time.

Transfer the Patterns:

1. Use a *dry* iron set at wool setting.

2. Place the fabric on the ironing board, right side up.

3. Cut out the desired motifs, allowing a margin around the edges of the design. Pin the design to the fabric with the printed side down. Place the pins through the margins to hold the transfer in place on the fabric. Protect the iron by placing a sheet of tissue paper between the transfer and the iron.

4. Place the heated iron on the transfer and hold down for about 5 seconds. Apply a firm, downward even pressure to all parts of the design, being especially careful to get the outer edges, such as the tips of leaves and flowers. Do not move the iron back and forth across the fabric as this will cause the transfer pattern to blur. After the transfer has been used once, apply iron for 2–3 seconds longer for each additional transfer.

5. Carefully remove one pin and lift one side of the transfer paper to see whether the complete design is indicated on the fabric. If not, replace the pin and repeat the process, concentrating on the area that did not transfer. Do not remove all the pins until you are sure the design has been successfully transferred. Once the pattern has been unpinned it is almost impossible to register it to the fabric again.

6. When you are satisfied that the transferring has been completed, unpin the transfer paper and peel it off. You will want to save the transfer paper to use for additional repeats (you can usually get four or more transfers from each pattern) or to use as a check on the design. If the design is not clear enough, you can refer to the transfer sheet and reinforce vague areas on the fabric with a waterproof laundry marker. Make sure that the ink is com-pletely waterproof because just the moisture from a steam iron can cause the ink to run and ruin your embroidery.

Special Instructions for Use on Dark Fabrics. If you wish to use these patterns on dark fabric on which transfer ink will not show up, or if you need additional repeats of the same transfer, put a piece of tracing paper over the uninked side of the transfer and trace the design. Discard the original transfer paper and pin the tracing in place on the fabric. Slip a piece of dressmaker's carbon, color-side down, between the fabric and the tracing; do not pin the carbon. With a hard, even pressure, trace a few lines with a tracing wheel, stylus or similar tool. Raise one corner of the tracing and the carbon to check the impression. If the results are too faint, apply more pressure; if too heavy, less pressure. After adjusting the impression, trace the entire design and then remove the carbon and carefully remove one pin to see whether the design is intact on the fabric *before removing the pattern.*

IMPORTANT

Since these transfer patterns are made to be used more than once, the ink will not readily wash out of the fabric. It is therefore important that the embroidery cover all transfer markings.

Notes on the plates appear after transfer patterns.

PLATE 1

PLATE 2

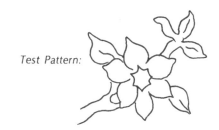

PLATE 3

PLATE 4

PLATE 5

PLATE 6

PLATE 7

PLATE 9

(1)

(2)

(3)

(4)

(5)

PLATE 8

Test Pattern:

PLATE 9

PLATE 9

Test Pattern:

PLATE 10

PLATE 11

Test Pattern:

PLATE 12

PLATE 13

PLATE 13

PLATE 14

Test Pattern:

PLATE 15

PLATE 16

PLATE 17

PLATE 18

Test Pattern:

PLATE 19

Test Pattern:

PLATE 20

PLATE 21

Test Pattern:

PLATE 22

PLATE 23

PLATE 24

Notes on the Plates

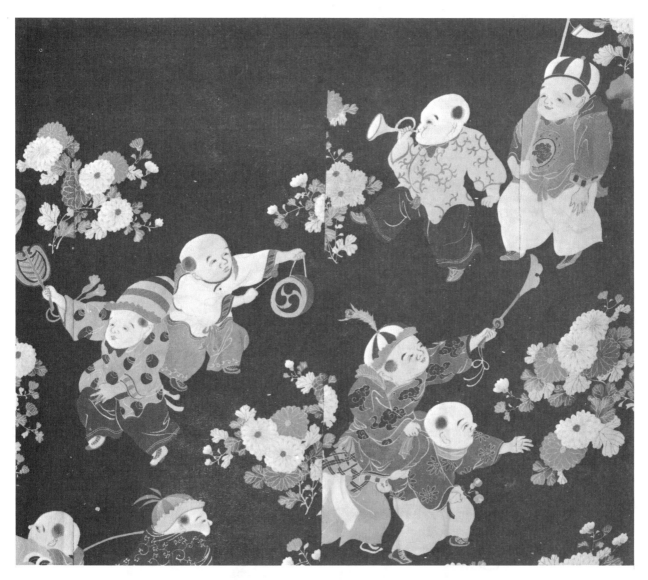

Plates 1, 2 and 3

The Japanese children playing are found on a black kimono (possibly a wedding garment, T.M.1973.12.5) attributed to the Taisho period. It is of special interest to embroiderers because, although the children were painted with a technique known as *yuzen,* needlework stitches are used throughout to provide textured details and highlights.

The painted areas are strong in color impact. The trumpeter wears blue pants, a yellow top with a visible green lining, a green scarf and green shoes. The flag boy is equally colorful with white pants, green-black shoes, and a mauve and white jacket patterned with beige and white and with a cheerful red lining. There are also children with green tops, gold pants and green shoes, and others wearing grey with mauve and blue details. The gong is bright red; the tassels and striped caps, vivid and cheerful in their color combinations.

To counter this liveliness, the scattered flowers are muted; their delicate green leaves shimmer at the tips with gold-worked satin stitches. The flowers are white, white and gold, soft blue and a soft tangerine. Within the flowers are tiny silk knots worked in the French manner and an occasional stitch here and there to accentuate a petal or detail.

Since the figures were originally painted, it would not be inappropriate to work them with long and short stitch and satin stitches, using stem and knots as dress details for a child or on a blouse. If outlines only are worked, small details such as lining, shoes, hair or toys should be worked in satin stitch for greater emphasis.

The figures on plates 1 and 2 are one-fourth the original size. The detail reproduced on plate 3 is approximately full size.

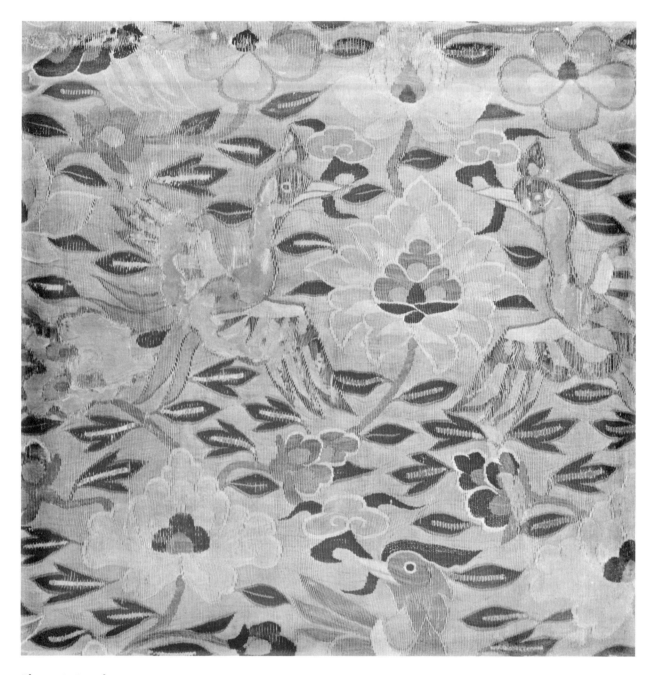

Plates 4, 5 and 6

The designs on these plates are all taken from the woven cover of a Chinese handscroll from the Sung Dynasty, 960–1279 (T.M.51.61). Silk tapestry weaving (*k'o-ssu*) was one of the great arts of the Sung Dynasty and included woven reproductions of paintings.

This handscroll cover is densely populated with flying birds holding a *ling chih* (fungus) amidst peonies and other blossoms. Gilded strips, originally brilliant, are visible in the leaves.

For practical present-day use, details from the scroll have been redrawn. Instead of one design showing two ducks flying from east to west, we give two separate motifs. The designs can thus be used as reversed single motifs for a pair of embroidered pillows. Additional duck motifs are provided for embroidered details or a personally arranged sequence of flying birds.

Closely worked parallel lines of stem, chain, split stitch or couched gilt threads would emphasize the simple double curves on silk or crewel work. To define each segment, outline it with a color other than the shade used in the central area.

In the original the following colors are used:

Peonies. Outer petals outlined in white, middle area in pale gold, centers white; inner petals outlined in white, middle area blue with gold centers.

Bird (Plate 4). Dark outlines, soft gold wings, beige, brown and white details, body of soft pale brown.

Bird (Plate 5). Soft grey-blue outlines, white body, indigo-blue wings with wide white wingspan.

Plate 7

Of special interest to embroiderers is this transfer from a fragment of a Uchikake robe from Japan of the Edo period, 18th century (T.M.52.8), possibly part of a robe worn by privileged ladies. The transfer is three times larger than one original repeat unit.

The scattered circles of the central flower, possibly a chrysanthemum, are the result of tie-dying rather than embroidery. Only the outline of each petal is worked in stem stitch. The adjoining flowers are worked in solid satin stitch with soft tangerine silk floss. The foliage is moss-green, veined with deep blue-green straight stitches, and the background surface is interspersed with bands of gilt.

Only superb craftsmanship and a demanding, affluent client could assure such perfect interaction of three textile techniques.

Plate 8
There are many symbolic *mon* or crest motifs in Japanese heraldry. In the past, within the rigid caste system of Japanese society, every family was entitled to the use of a mon. Important families were entitled to the use of two—one for formal occasions of importance, another for everyday use.

The mon symbol indicated family, caste, membership in a clan, a profession or trade. On her wedding day, a bride would wear a formal kimono, known as a *montsuki*, a gift from the groom's family with his crest either painted, embroidered or woven into the fabric. The Japanese custom of gift wrapping required a mon on the colored cloth which covered the gift. The wrapping would later be returned to the donor. In an affluent family, such wraps, known as *furoshiki*, would be elaborately embroidered with gold on heavy silk. In villages a dye-resist technique would stamp a mon on handwoven cotton cloth.

If the mon motif was totally embroidered, satin stitch (flat or padded) was used to fill all details. Sometimes the design was outlined by couched gold threads. The choice of a silk floss rather than gold embroidery thread as well as the background color was always based upon a family's tradition.

The five mon motifs on plate 8 show some botanical symbols commonly associated with the Far East.

Chrysanthemum flowers and leaves (1 and 2). More than one hundred different versions of this flower were used by the numerous princely family branches entitled to the chrysanthemum motif as their mon. These designs are especially interesting because they show how the ancient artists rearranged individual petals to achieve differences. The most stylized chrysanthemum crest is that of Japan's Imperial Family.

Bamboo (3 and 4). In Oriental art bamboo is generally shown as graceful and slender foliage on straight stalks; however, as a mon motif, where it serves as a crest design, it is rigid and firm.

The Lotus (5). Petals and leaves are stylized to conform to a circular shape.

Plate 9
The peonies on this plate are details from a woven Japanese Buddhist priest's robe or *kesa*, of brocaded, patched satin and faded red background coloring (T.M.1973.9).

Contrary to European custom, Japanese priestly garments were not shaped from large pieces of material. Instead, the valuable woven brocade was first cut into patches and then reassembled to symbolize Buddha's poverty. The most skilled of craftsmen were able to enrich the light-reflecting properties of the brocade and the design by careful rearrangement of the patches.

The Museum's *kesa* is unusual in that two different designs were used. One of peonies is woven with gold; the other of three-toed dragons is woven with a flat-strap silver thread. The peony design, which is reproduced here, has been redrawn to show several different positions so that an embroiderer can create an individual multiple arrangement of this lovely flower.

Plates 10 and 11
For more than 2,000 years the chrysanthemum has been cultivated in the Orient, and its graceful petals and lovely coloring have inspired the artists and craftsmen of Japan as well as China.

The chrysanthemums in these transfers are taken from a grey silk Chinese "Spanish" shawl. During the first two decades of this century the fashion for "Spanish" shawls exceeded production. Carefully embroidered in China, for export, with silk on silk and intricately fringed, they were worn in the West as evening wraps or displayed as grand piano covers.

Each motif of this sleeveband was worked with Peking knots (324 to the inch) in three shades of blue, reminiscent of export china, and outlined with couched gold threads.

The large natural blooms and blossoms of these motifs are embroidered with satin stitch for the petals, French knots for the centers and stem stitch outlines for the stalks. One pair of diagonally opposite corners is worked in shades of pale pink, apricot and scarlet, with the centers in dull green and red—the embroiderer having threaded both colors into one needle. The other corners have white, pale yellow, dull gold and deep gold flowers.

Plates 12 and 13
Pictures of a traditional Chinese landscape or garden have been familiar to every Westerner since the arrival of the first bulk shipments of chinaware at European and American ports. Strange pavilions with tapered roof lines were clearly marked in shades of blue on a white background. Shallow, covered boats floated along streams whose banks were shadowed by graceful pines and willow trees. Inevitably, curiously narrow and upward-curving structures bridged the water, and bats flew among the peonies and sacred fungus.

This pattern, adapted from the embroidered sleeve bands of a Chinese robe is typical of these traditional designs. Embroidered or *k'o-ssu* sleeve bands were often the most expensive part of non-court robes and were commissioned at the local embroidery workshop. Once a robe was soiled and worn, the sleevebands were removed and remounted onto a new robe. These embroidered sleevebands were considered to be part of a family's wealth and were handed down from one generation to the next.

Plates 14–21

The motifs in these plates are all adapted from a late 19th century Chinese Cloud Collar (T.M.1973.7.3). From time immemorial, collars—whether of fine metal, precious jewels, lace or fine embroidery—have been a valued and decorative detail of clothing. The collar in the museum collection is not only of elegant proportions, design and coloring, but its use of such symbols as insects, magnolias, peonies and *Ling Chih* can be read as wishes for long life, happiness, love, affection, prosperity, beauty, sweetness and even courage. It is tempting to spec-

ulate as to who wore it, who gave it and who commissioned it.

The workmanship is both graceful and perfect in the stitch placement of satin, long and short, Chinese knot details and couched parallel lines. The predominating colors are shades of blue and green with gilt used for the foliage. (The Chinese and Japanese use of gilt embroidery threads never overwhelms a design but instead tends to off-set the shaded areas.)

9

Plates 22, 23 and 24

The dragon robe of a Chinese Prince of the First Rank in the museum collection (T.M.1973.30.1) served as the source of these transfers. For thousands of years, the formality of Chinese life was carefully regulated. Fashion was only relevant in the refinement of ancient skills and traditional designs. The four to five years it took a workshop to finish a court robe was inconsequential. Only its ultimate beauty was important.

The background of the original is a dull-red silk gauze. The open mesh weave, known as leno, controls the stitches since every stitch enters or resurfaces through one of its holes, as in modern canvas work. The predominant stitch used is the encroaching satin, but there are details filled with long and short stitch, slanted stem stitch and couching. The stitch surface is flat, the emphasis being on the detailed design and colors.

The dragon reproduced on plate 24 is predominantly blue and is unusual because there is no gold work. The scales within the body are in shades of blue, each scale has three or four shades. The direction of the long and short stitches moves in the same direction as the scale is drawn. The top scales outlining the dragon are worked in a strong set of red shades while the scales outlining the inner curve and the undulating line at the tail are worked in white. The claws are dark blue; the flames spewing out of the mouth are coral; the tongue is red.